D0592518

your 14th ♡
Anniversary

The Romance of The Kiss

Compiled by
Suzanne Beilenson

Illustrated by Susan Zulauf

PETER PAUPER PRESS, INC.
WHITE PLAINS, NEW YORK

For Rob

Copyright © 1996
Peter Pauper Press, Inc.
202 Mamaroneck Avenue
White Plains, NY 10601
All rights reserved
ISBN 0-88088-793-1
Printed in Hong Kong
7 6 5 4 3 2 1

Introduction

Some people rub noses. Others brush eyelashes. Most just touch lips. No matter how you do it, though, a kiss expresses all the love, caring, tenderness, and passion between you and that special someone. So celebrate the delight and deliciousness of kissing with this little treasury of quotes. And then be sure to share them with your favorite pair of lips!

S. B.

Kisses are the language of
love, so let's talk it over.

American Proverb

The sound of a kiss is not
so loud as that of cannon,
but its echo lasts a great
deal longer.

Oliver Wendell Holmes

A kiss can be a comma,
a question mark or an
exclamation point. That's
basic spelling that every
woman ought to know.

Mistinguette

You are always new.
The last of your kisses was
ever the sweetest . . .

John Keats

All the legislation in the
world will not abolish
kissing.

Elinor Glyn

Stephen's kiss was
    lost in jest,
Robin's lost in play,
But the kiss in Colin's eyes
Haunts me night and day.

Sara Teasdale,
The Look

I'd like to kiss you, but I just washed my hair.

Spoken by Bette Davis, in *Cabin in the Cotton*

It was half past kissing
time, time to kiss again.

James Joyce,
Ulysses

No, I don't think I will kiss you—although you need kissing badly. That's what's wrong with you. You should be kissed and often and by someone who knows how.

Spoken by Clark Gable, in
Gone with the Wind

Two people kissing always
look like fish.

Andy Warhol

Where words cease, music begins, and where music ceases, kissing begins.

Norman Douglas

Two persons who do not
part with kisses should
part with haste.

Ralph Bergengren

A long, long kiss—the kiss
of youth and love.

Lord Byron

Few men know how to
kiss well; fortunately,
I've always had time to
teach them.

Mae West

That's the great thing about Hollywood: they have stunt kissers. At least that's what she told me.

Clint Black,
about his wife, Lisa Hartman Black,
filming love scenes

Kiss is like candy. You eat candy for the beautiful taste and this is enough reason to eat candy.

Spoken by Signe Hasso, in
Heaven Can Wait

The first kiss is the last you
see of your heart.

When they kissed it
seemed as if they did
indeed imbibe each other,
as if each were wine to the
other's thirst.

Robert Speaight,
The Unbroken Heart

Some women blush when
they are kissed, some call
for the police, some swear,
some bite. But the worst are
those who laugh.

William Raye

My child, if you finally
decide to let a man kiss
you, put your whole heart
and soul into it. No man
likes to kiss a rock.

Lady Chesterfield

Teach not thy lip such scorn,
for it was made
For kissing, lady, not for
such contempt.

William Shakespeare,
Richard III

When you get married you
forget about kissing other
women.

Pat Boone

A kiss must last long to be enjoyed.

Greek Proverb

Cynthia .. oh, she'll let you kiss her whenever you want. She doesn't want to swim. She doesn't want to play tennis, go for walks. All she wants to do is kiss you. I'm a nervous wreck!

Spoken by Mickey Rooney, in
Love Finds Andy Hardy

Between two pairs of lips
springs a river of love.

If I were what the words are,
And love were like the tune,
With double sound and single
Delight our lips would mingle,
With kisses glad as birds are
That get sweet rain at noon . . .

Algernon C. Swinburne

A woman should put
perfume on the places
where she wants to
be kissed.

Coco Chanel

What is a kisse? Why this,
   as some approve:
The sure sweet cement, glue,
   and lime of love.

Robert Herrick

You can't kiss a girl unexpect-
edly—only sooner than she
thought you would.

Jack Seaman

In love there is always one
who kisses and one who
offers the cheek.

French Proverb

This is one kiss you won't
be able to wipe off.

Spoken by Jean Arthur, in
The Plainsman

Any man who can drive
safely while kissing a
pretty girl is simply not
giving the kiss the
attention it deserves.

Evan Esar

How can distance make the heart grow fonder if kissing requires two people to be less than a millimeter apart?

Kiss me Kate, we will be
married o' Sunday.

William Shakespeare,
The Taming of the Shrew

It's even better when
you help.

Spoken by Lauren Bacall, in
To Have and Have Not

Kiss: a word invented by
the poets as a rhyme for
"bliss."

Ambrose Bierce

and there
is more
where that
came from

Let him kiss me with the
kisses of his mouth: for
thy love is better than wine.

Song of Solomon 1:2

There's never been anyone
to die because of a kiss, but
many a poor soul has died
for the lack of one.

American Proverb

And there I shut her wild,
  wild eyes
With kisses four.

John Keats,
La Belle Dame Sans Merci

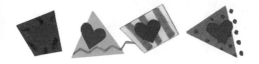

Kissing power is stronger
than will power: Girls need
to "prove their love" like a
moose needs a hat rack.

Abigail Van Buren

Kiss: a secret told to the
mouth instead of to the ear.

Edmond Rostand

The decision to kiss for the first time is the most crucial in any love story.

Emil Ludwig

When they kiss and make
up, she gets the kiss and he
gets the make-up.

Jacob M. Braude

A kiss is a lovely trick
designed by nature to stop
speech when words
become superfluous.

Ingrid Bergman

I wasn't kissing her, I was whispering in her mouth.

Chico Marx,
*when his wife caught him
kissing a chorus girl*

Something made of nothing,
  tasting very sweet,
A most delicious compound,
  with ingredients complete;
But if, as on occasion, the heart
  and mind are sour,
It has no great significance,
  and loses half its power.

Mary E. Buell,
The Kiss

When a boy steals a kiss,
Some cry foul, I say bliss.

Kiss: a thing of use to no
one, but prized by two.

Robert Zwickey

"May I print a kiss on your
    lips?" I said.
And she nodded her full
    permission;
So we went to press and
    I rather guess
We printed a full edition.

Joseph Lilienthal

Be touchable and kissable.

Marabel Morgan

If you want to kiss me any time during the evening, Nick, just let me know and I'll be glad to arrange it for you. Just mention my name.

F. Scott Fitzgerald,
The Great Gatsby

Speak, cousin, or, if you cannot, stop his mouth with a kiss.

William Shakespeare,
Much Ado About Nothing

Kiss: a pleasant reminder
that two heads are better
than one.

Rex Prouty

I say, when there are spats,
kiss and make up before
the day is done and live to
fight another day.

Rev. Randolph Ray

I am in favor of preserving the French habit of kissing ladies' hands—after all, one must start somewhere.

Sacha Guitry

You old mug. Take off your
shoes and kiss me.

Spoken by Claudette Colbert, in
The Gilded Lily

If you are ever in doubt as
to whether or not you
should kiss a pretty girl,
always give her the benefit
of the doubt.

Thomas Carlyle

People who throw kisses
are hopelessly lazy.

Bob Hope

A survey by Harlequin, a publisher of romance novels, found that Australian, German, Italian, and Japanese men said they keep the eyes closed when they kiss. A majority of American men said they keep their eyes open.

A compliment is something
like a kiss through a veil.

Victor Hugo

What of soul was left, I wonder,
when the kissing had to stop?

Robert Browning

A legal kiss is never as
good as a stolen one.

Guy de Maupassant

'Bout my first fella
I can hardly tell ya.
It's my first kiss
that I still do miss!

Nicole Beale

On the list of great inventions, kissing ranks higher than the Thermos bottle and the Airstream trailer; higher, even, than room service, probably because the main reason room service was created was so that people could stay in bed and kiss without starving.

Tom Robbins

A kiss may not be true, but
at least it's what we wish
were true.

Spoken by Steve Martin, in
L. A. Story

Rather an honest slap than
a false kiss.

Yiddish Proverb

Give me a thousand kisses,
then a hundred, then a
thousand more.

Catullus

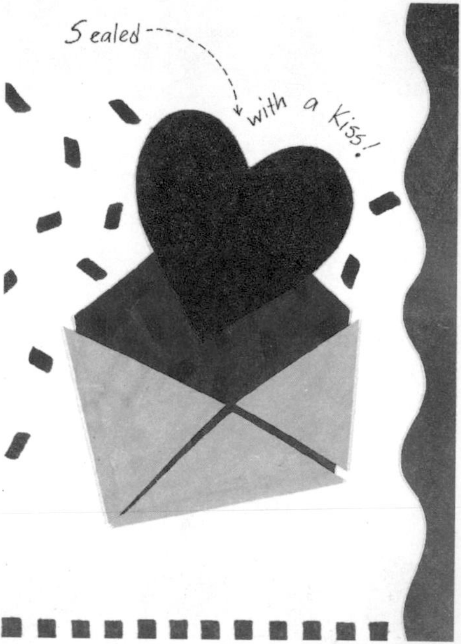
Sealed
with a Kiss!